UNTAMED
SEASONS

By Jessi Baird

words of a jay

ISBN: 9798844083204

acknowledgments

If I could personally thank
every person on social media
that pushed me to chase my
dreams… I would. To each
and every one of you: thank
you, truly.

To my sweet man: thank you
for holding my hand every
step of the way. While chasing
my dreams, you helped me see
that I am capable. You helped
me find bravery.

Fall

i'm wandering down an unfamiliar road
i hear the crunch of leaves beneath my feet
the sun is setting
spreading its vibrant colors across the sky
darkness will come soon
enveloping me in the only comfort i know
i wonder where this road will take me

how do i put
my thoughts on paper
for you to understand
when they don't even
make sense
in my own head

i often imagine
that you scan every crowd
and search for my face
because even after all this time
i can't help but do the same
i find myself
subconsciously hoping to see you
everywhere i go
because i know that
if our eyes were to meet
there would be a brief moment
of feeling like i was home

my entire being
is exhausted
i am so tired
of missing you

when
did i stop
making you happy?

places i would rather be than here:
watching a sunrise from the hillside
in a car singing my favorite songs
stargazing in an open field
seated next to a bonfire
barefoot on the beach
exploring a new city
anywhere but here
anywhere else

things i wanted to share with you:
morning coffee
walks with no destination in mind
road trips to find the next sunset
your last name

i wanted a forever
with who you were
in the very beginning
where did he go?

while i took
your hand
you took me
for granted

i tell everyone
that i'm fine
but i'm not
i'm far from fine

it's 3:17pm on a random tuesday
i wonder what you're doing
for no particular reason
other than the fact that
i miss you terribly

do you ever
dream about
what could have been?

i'm tired of temporary loves
unfinished chapters
i long for the
front porch
and rocking chairs
kind of love

tonight i miss you
more than normal
i picture your face
the smile that is
no longer directed at me
you aren't here anymore
so i write you into existence
through the words
i pour onto each page

did the promises
you made me
only feel right
that night?

we wished
on the same shooting star
i can't help but wonder
if this is what
you wished for

i wrote so many stories
about you
about us
page after page
you took up my whole book
and me?
i was just a brief mention
in your narrative

i never imagined
there would be
a version of me
without you
me before you
me after you
i can't decide
which one of those two
that i like more
but one thing i am certain of
is that the version of me with you
will forever be my favorite

am i ever
in the back
of your mind?
do you ever hear
my name
and wonder
how i'm doing?

you used to write
songs about me
send paragraphs
affirming your love
i was so sure of
you and me
now all you've done
is written me off

i had convinced myself
that my heart has mended now
yet my eyes
still flood with tears
when i recall our memories
grief has a funny way of
sneaking up on you

it's been years
since we said goodbye
but some days
i still really miss
the bond we found
in each other
i miss having someone
who heard my every word
talked to me
instead of talking at me
hugged me everyday
filled my bedroom
with fresh flowers
gently held my heart
i miss having someone
who never caused me to doubt
the love we shared

you carried
a ring in your pocket
for weeks on end
waiting for the right time
i'm relieved
that the moment never came
because i wouldn't
have been able to bare
the look in your eyes
caused by the inevitable
slow shake of my head

one day you will be
a different person
than the man who loved me
you will have
new goals and daydreams
new stories to tell
that don't include me
anymore
i won't know you
and i don't quite know
how to cope with that

forever forgotten
a book collecting dust
would you please
pick me up
again

how did i not see
that your heart was closed
from the very start
you could have cautioned me
saved me from
unnecessary agony

how was i
supposed to know
the way you felt
if you didn't tell me
until it was too late

i will never forget
the way you smiled
in those early days
your nose would crinkle
laugh lines reflecting your joy
i will also never forget
your voice
in those last days
the way your tone changed
distracted
distant

i wish i had been brave enough
to tell you all the things
i had been thinking
the moment
you left

all i have left of you
in my possession
are photos
but you still live
inside my heart
every moment
of every single day

the story you created
about me
is so inaccurate
but i will no longer
defend myself
from deaf ears
you have made up
your mind
and sadly
it seems
you never knew me
at all

i remember so clearly
laying in that field
staring up at the sky
wondering why
the clouds weren't moving
i realized
that they didn't want to leave
either

i packed
my bags
today
you forgot
to ask me
to stay

we fell apart
you never looked back
i can't look away
we weren't supposed
to end this way

i guess it wasn't
supposed to work out
we simply weren't
meant to be
i wanted you
you wanted to be free

you weren't there
the days that i felt
like i couldn't breathe
and that they
were never going to end
the nights that i could not
pick myself up
off the floor
you were not there
and i will not forget that

the room that
we created to be
our sanctuary
feels empty
cold
there's a void
bringing life back
into these walls
is a possibility
that only you hold

you said
it's all or nothing
i gave you my all
you gave me nothing
i guess
i have a habit of
misunderstanding

we stand before each other
every memory
we created
playing through my mind
i thought i was done
with goodbyes

people warned me about you
from the very start
but i still wrote your name
in bold letters across my heart
why did i give you my everything
when all you gave me was lukewarm love
they said you were inherently unhappy
yet i chose to believe
that i would be something special
someone that would bring you joy
you proved them right
and proved me wrong

you hurt me
i hurt you
our wounded hearts
threw scathing words back and forth
not knowing the years of hurt
they would cause
endless echoes on loop
of the things we didn't mean to say
the words that brought us to an end
i wish i could take back
every indignity that fell from my mouth
i wish the endless scoldings that you gave me
wouldn't haunt me every night

if i had to pick
a favorite time of year
i would choose the end of fall
right when our surroundings start to shift
changes that the universe makes for us
a feeling of bittersweet heaviness
while kissing the crimson colors goodbye
perhaps i feel the most comfortable here
because i have spent many nights
laying on the chilled ground
just like those autumn leaves
and i've had to part ways
with too many beautiful things

i don't feel at home
in my own skin
anymore
i no longer
recognize myself
i yelled at you today
you acted surprised
you aren't allowed
to be startled
by the person
you turned me into

my chest is tightening
my vision is blurring
ears ringing
fingers numb
the walls are caving in
falling to my knees
i can't breathe

Winter

lately
all i can focus on
is each breath i take
because everything else
is too much
and i will suffocate

the birds won't stop singing
outside my window
greeting me each morning
as if they haven't noticed
that everything is dead

some days i am uninspired
i float from room to room
barely existing
a ghost
other days
i write until
my pen runs dry
pouring every feeling
onto paper
hoping it vanishes

i feel nothing
and everything
all at once
it's rather frightening

i once found myself
pretty
now all i see
is a girl
with vacant eyes
void of any sign of life

what didn't
kill me
isn't making me
stronger

i want to tell our story
i just don't know
where to start
and i still don't know
where it ended

sometimes i whisper your name at night
wondering if you can hear me
if you can sense my pain
in the trembling of my voice
i plead for your return
as if my existence
depends on it

i wish
i could have shared
just one more
sunrise
with you

what could i have done
to have you love me
just a little bit longer?

after all these years
i still carry hope
that one day
you will look back
on the time that
you spent with me
and you'll see that everything
that you said you wanted
was standing
right in front of you
arms wide and heart open
selfishly i hope
that realization
brings you back to my door

i tried to hide my tears
on the last day that i saw you
i didn't want you to know
that our goodbye
was going to kill me too

what do you feel
when you think of me
does your heart swell with love
do you still see the future
that we daydreamed of
or do you see
me in your rear-view window
my voice just an echo
slowly fading away

i tend to resort to
self-sabotage
simply because
i don't believe
i'm worthy
of happiness

your eyes were made
to see straight through
the façade of me
you saw that behind my full smile
hid a hollow girl
i packed up overnight
left without a note
i needed to get far away
you deserve an explanation
i hope this is enough
i had never felt so seen
and that terrified me

the song you sang
words full of love
strung together
just for me
i sat in the crowd
your eyes stuck on mine
my heart
was already long gone

today i wiped my phone clean
gone is every trace of you
i threw away
everything that held
memories of us
i donated the pile of clothing
that you left in my closet
but now my problem is
i still can't get you
to leave my mind

all of my happiness
has drained from me
evaporated into thin air
like the morning dew

i wish i could reflect
on our days spent together
and smile
rather than fixate on
the ruins left behind us
i want to remember
you as love
instead of heartbreak
i want to remember
you resting your head in my lap
the way your eyes could always read mine
how you proudly called me yours
i don't want to remember
you telling me
that i came with too much baggage
and that you were looking
for someone better

wrapped in your arms
you told me that i was safe
i never saw the signs
of a wolf in sheep's clothing

you wrote me a song
a lyric still
trapped in my head to this day
'pretty as a painting'
did you not see
that my colors were bleeding
you fool
you only saw me in the way
that you wished i had been painted

i bury myself
under every blanket
trying to escape
the chill
i'm shaking
shivering
you used to
keep me warm
promising to
always build us a fire
now you've left me
to fend for myself

sometimes i wish you had
never loved me
so that way
i wouldn't hurt this badly

our love
was always a grenade
waiting
for the pin to be pulled free

i knew
that you would maim me
but my head
forgot to tell my heart

i kept all my flaws hidden
from you
when that's what needed love
the most
and when i finally showed you
all of me
that's when you chose
to leave

was it your intention
to make me
hate myself?

i told myself
to write something happy
paste a smiling face
over those acidic tears
i kept your verbal abuse
a secret
i didn't repeat the words
you kept cutting me with
your razor-sharp anger
hidden to all
because i knew
that i was too weak to leave

i said that i was afraid
and yet i told you
all my truths
i showed you
all my scars
we shared tears
secrets and stories
i gave you my shoulder
to rest your tired mind
and then you went
straight for the jugular

your tongue of cruelty
were nails in the coffin
your words were shrapnel
and i was in the line of fire
yet i still wanted more
of you
i wonder what is wrong
with me

you tore me apart
piece by piece
fooling everyone
disguising it as love
all the while
my remaining
tattered fragments
were begging
for someone to see
the mess you had made
of what was left of me

i hope you die alone
(five words you said to me)
a waste of time
(four words you shouted at me)
stop being annoying
(three words you told me)
fuck you
(two words you spat at me)
useless
(one word you called me)

your cold heart
and brutal words
crushed my fragile bones
one by one
you saw the damage
you continuously caused
tossed out an empty apology
and never made any change

you had so many
complaints
about me
it always left me
wondering
if there was anything
you loved
about me

it sickens me
that you never wanted
to provide me of
a secure love
a safe place
a home
and yet i still stayed
desperately offering you
my futile heart

did you ever love me at all
or did you just love
the idea of loving me
eventually discovering that
i have never been any good at
being good enough

how humiliating it is
to have to beg someone
to tell you
what they like
about you
the shame you feel
staying
when you know
that you deserve better

i sit in the shower
a little longer lately
just to feel
some form of warmth

ten fingers
ten toes
i wonder if
you had my nose
now you are
somewhere above
i hope you can feel
mommy and daddy's love

i am sorry that i failed you
your heart stopped
within my body
that was the day
my heart stopped too

i didn't think
i would ever live
in a world where
you aren't here
i don't want
life to carry on
like this

maybe you were
in desperate search
to find evil within me
in order to justify
the evil within yourself

my hands are turning blue
i don't know how long
i have been standing
out in this bitter cold
i wonder
how long it takes
for someone
to freeze to death

i was in the deep end
drowning
i called out your name
begging for help
you saw me
and walked away
i'm slowly sinking

i gave you
everything
i could think of
silly of me
to think
that would be
enough

i can't say that i want revenge anymore
my anger has dissolved
however i can't help but hope
that you carry a sense of guilt
for slowly tearing me to shreds
leaving no signs of life
hiding your dangerous nature
behind closed doors
laughing at my tears
eyes full of hatred
i had been proud of myself
before you came around
today i have decided
that it is time to
start working on
getting back to the old me

i have accepted that
not every
'once upon a time'
ends with a
'happily ever after'

i let go of you
the person i kept in my mind
i blinked
and you disappeared
i painfully bid you farewell
because i know
that i'm never going to heal
while clinging to you

Spring

today i took note
of new life flourishing
the wildflowers making
their yearly grand entrance
i sense that they are whispering to me
that it is time to let myself heal
to do the work
start fresh and blossom
there is nobody stopping me
other than myself

life touched my lungs
i inhaled it deeply
choosing in that moment
to embrace my past
my pain and my disappointments
that breath of fresh life
travelled from my lungs
to my bones
slowly i am mending my wounds
and i will soon be free

to the next person who loves me:
all i want to say is
please be gentle with me

i don't know
how long i had been
holding my breath
clenching my jaw
but i am learning
how to exhale again
and my god,
what a relief
it is

you stole
my voice
and wrote
your own story
i am taking
the pen back

i finally see it now
i never needed
your love
i just wanted it

i took a seat
in the back row
of my life
for too long
allowing myself to become
a wallflower
i am taking center stage again
i am stepping back
into the main character role

it took me years
to discover
that you don't
determine my worth

i finally chose me
over you
i deserve that

a letter to me:
i am sorry for
not loving you
in the way that
you deserved

every inch of me
is worthy
of my own love

dear past me,
i wish i had loved you better on those days that you could not get up off the ground instead of shaming you. i wish i had given you permission to take time to heal; i wish i had not forced you to smile and assure others that you were okay when you weren't. i wish that i hadn't made you pour every ounce of your love into people who wouldn't give you anything in return. i am sorry.
i am so sorry.
love,
today me

you taught me
that not everything
is worth fighting for
i won't lose myself
trying to win you

it hurt so badly
to let you go
but i needed to
in order to grow
holding on to you
was going to kill me

you packed me away
in a box
tied up with a pretty bow
honey,
there's a new version of me
and i have outgrown the space
you confined me in

our love was beautiful
and even if we weren't
meant to be
thank you
for loving me
in the only way
that you knew how

we don't speak
anymore
but my heart
still loves
your heart

you will always have
a piece of me
but i will no longer
let you
steal my joy

i stopped begging for your love
i wiped my hands clean of you
i started giving myself the love
that i so desperately needed
i was never enough for you
but i am enough for me

i replaced complacency
with consistency
i replaced aimlessness
with intention
and with this
i am watching
my life
transform

what i bring to the table
will be exactly what someone
is looking for
but in the meantime
i have found serenity
in this table set for one
because what i have to offer
is perfectly enough for me

i'm not bothered by you
anymore
i have finally spotted the lies you fed me
leading me to doubt my self-worth
i picked apart fact from fiction
and i am reclaiming my value

i believed
i had to have
someone by my side
i have become to love
the empty chair
next to me
confident that one day
it will be filled
by someone who
feels like daylight

i will find someone
who sees my flaws
that you've deemed scars
to be ashamed of
and that someone
will trace those old wounds
listening to every story
seeing bravery in each injury
and instead of holding mc hostage
to my past
will love me more
because of my resilience

i used to wonder
why i had to endure
all the trials
sent my way
i see it clearly now
it was for me to share
and lift up
the stranger who needs
encouragement

i believe that my words
will carry you
to a different place
a place that fills you
with promise
and motivation

i hope you come to find
that you don't have to stay
with what is comfortable
the future you planned out
can be rewritten

you gave it
all you could
fought until the final straw
broke the camel's back
it wasn't your fault
i promise

there will be happiness
after this sorrow
first kisses that taste like sunshine
coffee brewed just the way you like it
a breeze on your face that brings a soft smile
there will be days
that you will be grateful
for pushing forward
when all you wanted to do
was collapse

endings
always lead
to new beginnings

there is a freshly planted garden
waiting to bloom within your heart
please don't forget to water it

right now
you are under construction
you owe no one an explanation
for choosing to take the steps
in the direction that will
help you feel alive again

please do not
undermine yourself
you are not a damsel
in distress
in need of someone
to save you
you have everything it takes
to be your own savior

always make room
in your life
for people who
make room
for you

sometimes
you must sit
in the dark
on those days
i will sit with you
and together
we will wait
for the new light

the days that you're tired
carrying pain that you believe
will never subside
just remember these words:
one day
you will look back
from the destination
you have arrived at
and it will all make sense
the weight on your back
was there to strengthen you
on your journey
not to hold you down

you loved them
with your entire heart
and maybe you still do
but did you know that
you can love yourself
that way too?

here's a disclaimer:
if you find yourself wondering
if you deserve better
than what they are giving you
i can assure you
that you do

do you miss them
or just the romanticized
version of them?
remember the good days together
but do not ignore the bad days

they broke you
and then they left you
but the person
you are becoming?
that person will stay with you
forever
always evolving and growing
so be kind to yourself
as you adjust
to your new normal
as you transform
into the stronger you

right now
you're hurting
you feel lost
sweet soul,
you are not alone
and no matter what you do
don't give up
don't stop searching
for yourself

your every tear
has its own story
and honey,
i want to hear them all

you may have been broken
but you are not incomplete
the pieces are all still there
it's time to dust yourself off
pick up those shards of you
and recreate yourself
into a mosaic masterpiece

never sacrifice
your peace
for what feels
comfortable
never settle
for what feels
familiar

don't let your mind
trick you
into thinking
you aren't worth it

you are not defined
by your lowest moments
your worst days
the mistakes you made
along the way
you are defined by
the days that you spent
fighting for your life
crawling through the darkness
not knowing if you would make it
but choosing to inch forward
you are defined by
your perseverance
your courage
your bravery

you are changing
and that is beautiful
you have kept yourself
in a cage
for too long
you are growing
soon you will see
that you have wings
and you will soar

you are worth it
everything that you long for
write that
on your mirror
until it is etched
into your heart

i hope you laugh
until your sides hurt
i hope you love
with all your heart
i hope you choose
to live a meaningful life

you are limitless
the sky is not
big enough
for you

you are allowed
to break down
you are allowed
to have bad days
you are allowed
to ugly cry
you are allowed
to not be okay
just remember that
one day
the sun will shine again
these days
won't last forever

the mountain
that you are climbing
will soon become
a memory
a badge of honor
displaying your
unwavering endurance

have the fearlessness
to ride out the waves
because the voyage
does bring smooth sailing
in the end
and when you finally drop anchor
you will see
that you weathered the storm
and came out
holding your head high

what are you
waiting for?
it is time
to shine your light
brighter than
ever before

Summer

there is no map
no compass or directions
but my heart
is on its journey home
to the place
that brings me nothing but
peace

i sat and watched you
an easy smile across your lips
your eyes dancing
i felt my once jaded heart
opening up
to the possibility of
loving again

things i find therapeutic:
mountain top views
the sound of rain
crashing waves
clean sheets
a new book
you

i do not carry my heart
on my sleeve
it's tucked away
instead
my fear is displayed
yet you were not deterred
by my guarded love

your fingers
gently tangled
in my hair
my heart
slowly falling
into your hands

we talk about the stars
our endless daydreams
my pinky entwined with yours
let's make those dreams
our reality

your untamed
wild vines
are growing
inside my heart

my life has consisted of a series
of good and bad events
but you, my dear
have made it all
make sense

let's run away
you and me

you don't remember
the day we met
you sat across from me
i was a face you would soon forget
you were a man
i knew fate would bring back
into my life
and fate sure did deliver
on the day i saw you again
your eyes met mine
i was greeted
with your winning smile
and that time
you didn't forget

you calmed
my frantic heart
you unraveled
my disarrayed thoughts
you saw all that i was
and still found me beautiful

it is raining outside
just like the day we ran
through the city streets
we huddled under a canopy
you stood close enough
that i could see the raindrops
clinging to your eyelashes
i am glad you forgot the umbrella

you kiss me on my nose
i feel it in my toes
this love has
flooded my bones

i am dazzled by the light
shining from your eyes
i am cloaked
in your tender love
you are the one
i have been waiting for

you
are
my
happy
place

lying in bed
you trace
those three words
into the palm of my hand
you brush my hair
away from my face
plant a kiss on my forehead
my heart
is so
full

i spilled coffee
on your white rug
habit took me back
anxiety bubbled through me
you smiled
picked me up
spun me around
told me
that my messy tendency
leaving my trace everywhere
was one of your favorite things
about me

i carry myself lighter now
i notice my surroundings
appreciating everything i see
there is a new spark
lit in my heart

you shower me
with such a pure love
eyes trained on mine
you speak every word
that i never knew i needed to hear
i see it in your eyes
each syllable
formed from your lips
hold the truth
i see that
you believe in me

let's throw away
our plans
and chase
the sunset

you always know
exactly what to do
when my heart
is beating out of my chest
when my panic starts setting in
when i can't form a coherent sentence
you recognize it before i do
you see me
you know me
and somehow
you still love me

you handed me a key
a twinkle in your eye
you want to share
your space
with me
falling, falling
i am falling
for you

let's stay in bed
listen to the sound
of the rain
let's have breakfast
at midnight
i like it better
when the stars are out
anyway

your lips lingered
so close to mine
that when you smiled
i felt it

you brought me
a sigh of relief
my heart didn't know
it needed

hand in mine
you took me
by surprise
when you whispered
that you loved me
i will never know
what you see in me
but i hope
you never stop

carved your name
into my heart
forever it will stay
what an exquisite
piece of art

it appears that
i found my other half
when i no longer needed
another half

sitting on that hill
surrounded by daises
you ventured there
each spring
this time
you have taken me
with you
you are showing me
your world
i am enchanted by it

my sweet love
just for tonight
can we forget
the world
and dance
with the stars

i am caught off guard
by the way
our souls are aligned
i never knew
a connection like this
existed
i can't wrap my mind
around my luck

our hearts
have crafted
a language
of their own
spoken only
to each other

the universe
reminds me of you
in every night sky
your name written
across the constellations

honey,
i will always be
your biggest fan

lately i have been picking
every dandelion i see
making the same wish:
that it will always be
you and me

you are the forever
that i am terrified to lose
i am scared that
history will repeat itself
even in love

i will cherish
even the
saddest version
of you

last night i dreamt of all our days
it was like watching a fairy tale movie
my heart is so full of love
but i could not help but observe
the slow fading of your smile

i remember when
you used to have
my coffee ready
every morning
today
i poured my own cup

you sit and stare
at your phone
i sit and stare
at your face
how did this
become
our new normal

you are slowly becoming
a stranger to me
i think i'm having
déjà vu

you always made sure
to make time for me
a priority
it hurts to see
that i don't fit
into your schedule
anymore

our slow mornings
bed head and hot coffee
i looked forward to this
each dawn
now you sleep late
our routine
was short lived
it's okay
rest your mind
i will wait until you wake
i will always wait

i am not sure when you stopped
asking how my day went
i can't pinpoint when you stopped
kissing me goodnight
i notice the crisp smell of fall coming
and i sense that you may be leaving
along with the warm season

our love in seven words:
like the summertime
it's ending too soon

you told me
not to compare you
to my last shattered love
or the one before that
but my dear
it is written on the walls
hidden in your every action

you are tired
of my tears
i am tired
of my confusion
please stop
sending me
mixed signals
either stay
or walk away

i recognize that
once again
i am afraid to share
my thoughts
so i am begging you
to hear the words
my eyes are
silently screaming

maybe i am delusional
i'm pretending
that i haven't seen this
happen before

i recognize it
i'm playing
the old game
the one where
i don't fight for
what i know i need

my love
deserves more
than the
bare minimum

i have to let you go
i have to remember
the pain of each
heartache
i have written about
i won't let myself
fall into that
pit of despair
once again

i say my final goodbye
it is time to bury
our memories
six feet under
right next
to the rest of the heartbreaks
you promised me
you wouldn't be like them
you promised me
you would always stay

almost
we almost
made it

i'm wandering down a familiar road
i hear the crunch of leaves beneath my feet
the sun is setting
spreading its vibrant colors across the sky
darkness will come soon
enveloping me in an old source of comfort
i know where this road will take me
maybe i should turn around

authors note

If you or a loved one is in need of help to better your mental health, I'd like to provide you of a few resources. I know how difficult it is to take the first step to seek help but I promise you: you can do it. You deserve to give yourself love and compassion by reaching out.

Find general support, services and treatment: www.nami.org

Crisis Lifeline:
Call 988
llame al 988 (para ayuda en español).

Crisis Textline:
Text "HELLO" to 741741.

author bio

Jess started writing down her thoughts over a decade ago; growing a collection of poems which caught the attention of over 200 thousand readers. She now tells these stories on Instagram sharing her journey of love, heartbreak, grief and healing.

Jess' mission is empowering others to embrace the ebb and flow of life. To remind them the days that feel the darkest are actually the days that mold them into their most courageous and joyous self.

Jess' passions are sobriety, mental health, self-love and taking the road less travelled. She enjoys people: listening, learning and loving.

While Jess resides just outside of Austin, Texas, you can usually find her curled up with a book, dreaming of her next adventure or chasing the days sunset.

You can follow Jess on all social media platforms as @wordsofajay.

Printed in Great Britain
by Amazon

33620212R00128